IF YOU'RE COMFORTABLE,
YOU'RE NOT GROWING

IF YOU'RE COMFORTABLE, YOU'RE NOT GROWING

FINDING YOUR TREMENDOUS

Dan Charles Pope

ISBN: 0692861343
ISBN-13: 9780692861349
Library of Congress Control Number: 2017904463
Dan Charles Pope, Paducah, KY

To my wife, Rebecca, who has always been my greatest cheerleader and supporter. To my three children, Cullen, Reid, and Addie, who make me want to be the best role model I can be. To my parents, Charles and Jacquie Pope, and to my brother David, who all helped make me who I am today. To my mother- and father-in-law, Richard and Jane Throgmorton. In addition, to Tom and Loraye Jones, who helped me discover many of the themes I've presented in this book through shared experiences and numerous conversations.

CONTENTS

INTRODUCTION

BEING COMFORTABLE IS great for new shoes or a pair of jeans, but it won't help you develop your skills as a leader. Living in your comfort zone will also prevent you from reaching your potential. Early in my career as a principal, I learned that staying in my comfort zone would prevent me from creating the best possible environment for my students and staff and from building a community that would know the importance of learning and growing.

I've had the opportunity to spend the last thirty-two years in public education, leading others in many different situations. I chose to be a different kind of leader, leading in the way I wanted other leaders to lead.

In July 2016, I retired and started to develop my new "significance." For my retirement, my faculty gave me a book titled *Intentional Living*, by John Maxwell. In this book, the author makes the point that leaders must share their ideas; he also talks about finding significance. As I made my transition from thirty-two years as an educator to the life of a retiree, finding my new significance, I knew that this would mean I'd have to share my experiences.

I want to lead in a completely different way and to continue to have a positive impact while helping others.

During my time as a principal, each year I would choose a theme that we would use to provide focus and to frame our school year. Each theme would focus on the needs of the staff, our school, and the students. The chapters of this book are based on the themes and lessons we all learned during those years as we collaborated with our school family.

Beginning with chapter 1, "Finding 'Tremendous,'" each chapter has a strong personal connection with its theme. Each theme encompasses the core beliefs that I've developed about leadership over the years. Each year, I'd look at the challenges our school community faced; by collaborating with others (including my wife), we'd then develop the theme.

I believe that everyone has an opportunity to be a leader, regardless of title, position, or place in life. One of the goals of this book is to help you develop your skills as a leader, regardless of your occupation and your leadership position (or lack thereof). As part of my new significance, I set a goal to write this book and pass on my experiences to others.

I want this book to help you find the leader within you. I want to lead you to find the motivation to develop your skills. I'll move you through my life as a leader and the experiences and lessons I learned along the way. I want you to recognize that if you're comfortable, you're not growing. Each chapter will help you develop your tool kit as a leader and will provide you with the motivation to leave your comfort zone. Because real leaders share their ideas and experiences with others, once you've finished this book, you must begin practicing and sharing what you've learned with the people you lead.

Finally, I hope to instill in you the belief that you can change the world. You can have a positive impact on others by giving freely, making changes, creating hope, setting goals, and leading others. These facets will all help to build the capacity for leadership in others.

CHAPTER 1

FINDING "TREMENDOUS"

*I'm not a genius. I'm just a
tremendous bundle of experience.*

—R. BUCKMINSTER FULLER

WHAT WE SAY as we talk to one another sets the tone for
how we greet the day. Our words determine how we interact with one another and can set the path for what words
others will communicate to us. Positive words matter.

In 1987, at the beginning of my third year as a teacher, we had an opening-day meeting for all teachers and
staff in the district. I signed in and made my way to the
doughnut table and then greeted the other teachers,
many of whom I hadn't seen since the last day of school.
As the time for the meeting approached and the moments of socializing came to an end, we were asked to
find our seats. I'd waited too long to find my seat, which
meant that I had few chairs to choose from. I settled on a
seat in the middle of the room and sat down.

A gentleman sitting beside me began to ask me questions. Assuming that he was a new teacher I politely answered his questions and began to carry on a conversation with him. The last question he asked me has permanently frozen the memory of this day in my mind. His question was simple. He asked me if I enjoyed these types of meeting. I responded with this statement: "Not really; we usually have to listen to a boring speaker instead of spending time in our classrooms. It's usually a waste of time." He looked at me and laughed. To paraphrase the late Paul Harvey, here is the rest of this story.

Our superintendent, Mr. Harper, stepped to the podium and introduced the speaker by providing a glowing list of experiences and qualifications. Then Mr. Harper said, "Let's welcome our speaker." The gentleman sitting beside me stood up, patted me on the back, and walked toward the podium. At that moment, everything I'd said to him quickly ran through my mind, especially the part about boring speakers. I was fortunate that he didn't say anything about our conversations, but what he did say would have a lasting effect on me for the rest of my career.

He was not a boring speaker. He told us an intriguing story about his life and his path to finding positivity. He encouraged each of us to choose a strong, positive word to use as a personal adjective. This word would display our positive approach to the day.

The word he'd chosen was *tremendous*. He went on to explain that when someone greeted him and asked him how he was doing, he would respond with "I'm doing tremendous" or "Today is a tremendous day." His point was that using positive words intentionally sets a positive tone.

He finished his motivational presentation, and we all made our way to our schools to begin the school year. I couldn't get his presentation out of my mind. I wanted to be that positive person whom he described and whom he modeled. I made the decision to use a positive word. For me, nothing other than the word *tremendous* seemed to fit.

I began to use *tremendous* as my personal adjective. It took some time, but by the end of my career, my staff knew that they would hear me use *tremendous* on a daily basis. If something occurred that was positive, I would somehow figure out how to use *tremendous* to praise, describe, or show my approval.

So what is your tremendous? What positive words do you use? Do you greet the day on a positive note? Where do you begin?

1. Start observing the words you use every day.
2. Before you speak, take a moment to think about what you're going to say.
3. Always try to use positive language, even when you're tempted to use words that could be interpreted in a negative manner.

4. Choose a positive personal adjective and add it to your daily dialogue.

5. Make the choice to speak in a positive tone and to use positive language. Remember that this is a choice.

CHAPTER 2

WORDS OF WISDOM

*When I was a boy of fourteen, my father was
so ignorant I could hardly stand to have
the old man around. But when I got to be
twenty-one, I was astonished at how much
the old man had learned in seven years.*

—MARK TWAIN

DURING THE LAST ten years of my career, I had the rewarding opportunity to be the principal at Lone Oak Elementary School in Paducah, Kentucky. The experiences I gained there were priceless. The relationships I built and the lessons I learned there will stay with me for the rest of my life. Those lessons are far too valuable for me to keep to myself and not to share with others.

Through my mentors and the motivational authors whom I've studied, I've developed the belief that leaders must share their "mountaintop" experiences and failures with others. I believe that sharing is an unwritten rule of leadership. Throughout the chapters of this book, it is my intent to share the various lessons that have shaped me as a leader.

I've played many leadership roles throughout my career as an educator. The role that had the most impact on me in developing my leadership philosophies was my role as principal. It was my dream job, and I cherish all the experiences I continue to carry with me to this day.

When you take on the role of principal, you are required to be an encourager and motivator for students, parents, and staff. You have to be a positive driving force. You must be realistic while maintaining a half-glass-full-mentality with any issues, situations, and circumstances that arise.

I made the commitment to be a different kind of leader. I'd worked with many leaders up to that point, but none had inspired me to be the best teacher I could be. I promised myself that when I had the opportunity to lead, I'd choose to be different. I'd remember the things that had often frustrated my fellow staff members and me. I would be the encourager I hoped to have had when I was a young teacher. I'd push my staff to reach beyond the status quo.

I also realized that if I wanted to attain success for students, staff, and parents, I would have to become an intentional motivator and a constant encourager: not just someone who dangled carrots and occasionally patted people on the back, but someone who really cared about others and genuinely encouraged and motivated them. I had to model this style of leadership, and I had to create a climate that would encourage and motivate everyone. It had to be an atmosphere that would lead people to reach their potential and embrace new ideas.

So my journey began with this belief: everyone is responsible for motivating, encouraging, and inspiring those they lead. I have confidence in that statement and have molded my vision as a leader around that belief. To take that idea further, I believe that motivating, encouraging, and inspiring are among the most important responsibilities of any leader. Without inspiration, leadership may just be based on power, fear, or dumb luck.

In the field of education, it is even more important to model motivation and encouragement than in other fields. If we want our teachers to motivate and encourage our students, then their leaders must model this behavior. That's right; leaders have the responsibility to model the characteristics they expect and want to see in their followers. If you look at any leaders, you'll find others modeling their leadership styles. Whatever the leaders model will eventually become part of the culture of the school or workplace. Even if their leadership style is weak or adverse, others will model it. That's why it's especially important to lead through motivation and encouragement.

I believe that certain foundational characteristics must be in place if you wish to have credibility so that you'll be able to motivate, encourage, and inspire staff, peers, and others. It took me a number of years and many experiences to create a set of foundational characteristics of leadership that would eventually help me achieve success.

I wanted to leave no stone unturned when my retirement as a school principal was approaching. I made sure that I gave everything I could that last year. I did more and worked harder than ever before. I didn't want anyone to say later that I hadn't done my best just because I was retiring. It was an emotional time for me, because I devoted every bit of energy I had to give my best.

During the last few weeks before my retirement, I began to reflect on what I'd experienced throughout my career. From that reflection, I knew that I wanted to leave my staff with what I called my thirteen words of wisdom. These thirteen words of wisdom are the foundational characteristics that I believe are paramount to leadership. They may be used for much more than just leadership; they are also words of wisdom for life.

1. *Relationships.* Significant relationships are the cornerstone of leadership. One of my favorite quotes is by professor of child psychiatry at Yale University, James P. Comer, who has stated that "no significant learning occurs without significant relationships." I believe that this philosophy can also be applied to leadership. Successful

leadership will not occur without significant relationships. If you study effective leaders, you'll find that they've mastered the ability to develop relationships. Whether you're in education or another field, success begins and ends with relationships, relationships, relationships, and relationships.

2. *Shout it from the rooftops. Praise and applaud often.* Honor the accomplishments of the members of your organization and family, both in private and in public. It is important that your praise is honest and meaningful. It has to be deliberate, consistent, and fair. Give people pats on the back daily. You must set aside time to create deliberate praise and celebrate your peers and organization. Don't be afraid to shout their praise from the rooftops.

3. *Dance, celebrate, and sing.* Celebrate the success of your organization; you must also recognize the personal hurdles and accomplishments of your team. Show them that you care about them personally. Celebrate together and often. Rejoice in their hard work and fortune, whatever it may be.

4. *Don't live for the weekend.* Every day of the week is important, and each day has its purpose. Make sure that you model daily significance. Remember, whatever you do today has significance; we just need to make sure it is a positive significance.

5. *Don't complain.* Complaining is the path to negativity. Complaining will not help you to be successful or lead you toward accomplishing things. A leader who complains will have an organization that complains. Know that we imitate our leaders.

6. *Remember that you are leaving a legacy.* Make sure that your legacy is a positive and productive gift that you're giving to your followers as well as the leaders whom you're mentoring. Model the importance of leaving a positive legacy, and make it clear that your current circumstances are an opportunity, not an obligation. (You'll read more about this in chapter 15.)

7. *Commit to being a lifelong learner.* If you're always learning, you're always growing. When we stop learning, we stop thriving. Be committed to learning every day.

8. *Move your own cheese.* Realize when you need to make personal changes before someone has to bring it to your attention. Don't let yourself get stuck in a career or personal rut. Learning to move your own cheese is a skill that is vital in leadership characteristics.

9. *Don't take yourself too seriously.* Your followers need to see that you are human. They need to see that you make mistakes and laugh at yourself as well as laugh with others. Make the decision

that your workplace will be a productive and fun environment.

10. *Do the right thing for the right reason.* Stand up for what is right. Keep integrity a priority by doing what is right. It's not always easy to be a leader who produces a positive impact, but you must stand up for what's right.

11. *You can't please everyone, so don't try.* The breakdown of an organization will inevitably occur when pleasing everyone comes before doing the right thing. You can't please everyone, so don't try.

12. *Be passionate about your job, and show compassion.* Everyone needs to see that you're passionate about what's important to you as a leader and what's important to the organization. Be enthusiastic, because it is contagious and because enthusiasm inspires people.

13. *Lead with your faith.* My faith has been my guide and my strength throughout my struggles and accomplishments. Most of my words of wisdom are connected to my faith in some way. Throughout my career, it was crucial to me that my decisions and my leadership would reflect my faith.

My experiences in leading and in developing other leaders led to the creation of this list. These tips came from both good and not-so-good experiences that all helped to frame my beliefs as a leader. They were my words of wisdom to my staff as I handed over my responsibilities to the new principal. I wanted to continue to have significance. I wanted to offer to others what I've learned from my experiences. The following pages and chapters reflect how I've tried to encourage, motivate, and inspire those who have chosen to follow me.

I challenge you as you continue to read to reflect and ask yourself these questions: Are you motivated at your job, at school, or wherever else you spend your day? Do you encourage others? Are you a motivator? Do others come to you for inspiration? Are you enthusiastic about your work? Do you inspire others on a daily basis? Do you seek significance?

I've often told my students that the word *encourage* means to place courage inside others. When you encourage others, you are giving them the gift of courage. When we encourage someone, we are giving him or her a gift. Once someone has encouraged you and given you the gift of courage, you have the responsibility to pass it on to someone else. That is the purpose of this book. I want to continue to be a positive driving force of encouragement. I choose to continue to be significant.

Once you've read this book, you will then have the responsibility to motivate, encourage, and inspire others. Join me in my goal of being a different type of leader.

Remember, once someone has encouraged you and given you the gift of courage, you have the responsibility to pass it on. Make that your significance.

CHAPTER 3

IF YOU'RE COMFORTABLE, YOU'RE NOT GROWING

Find your comfort zone and then leave.

—ANONYMOUS

THE SUMMER OF 2015 involved several days of traveling with my son to various baseball tournaments. On one particular trip, we found ourselves eating breakfast at McDonald's. As I sat waiting for my son to eat his breakfast, I observed three older gentlemen in the corner, passionately discussing their route for their morning destination. Two of the gentlemen had an accordion-folded Rand McNally map that they were scouring to find the best route. The other gentleman sat quietly observing his buddies on the other side of the booth until the conversation turned to the use of GPS rather than a reliable old gas-station glove-box map.

I listened as the third man tried to persuade his friends to use the GPS. He gave them many reasons to use GPS over the comfortable and less threatening road map. Then the other two gentlemen told him every reason that they should *not* use a GPS and why the old way was much better. Finally, he gave up on his attempt to move his friends into the era of GPS and let them go back to searching their glove-box map.

As I watched the conversation between these three older gentlemen, I thought about how change makes people react. Some are able to embrace change, while others run from it. How we handle change molds our success, and our reactions to change determine if we move forward or remain stuck in the same place. Most importantly, if we are leading, then others are waiting to see how we react when change takes place.

What I witnessed that morning is a battle that occurs in many workplaces, schools, and homes. We become comfortable with a routine, method, practice, or technique. We don't want things to change. We want things to be easy, and we especially want them to be comfortable. Unfortunately, comfort does not lead to change. Comfort is great for a new couch or chair or a family gathering but not for creativity, productivity, or a healthy mind. Especially in work fields such as education, being comfortable leads to boring routines and robotic lessons. Students are the ones who receive that sour fruit of being comfortable. It has the same effect in any workplace situation: comfort zones lead to complacency.

Early in my career as an elementary school principal, I wanted to effect change. As I discussed earlier, I believed that as a leader, it was my responsibility to provide encouragement, motivation, and inspiration to those whom I led. Eager to find ways to motivate and encourage, I began to study authors such as Wooden, Maxwell, and Sanborn as well as many others. It was a trip with my family to Lake Cumberland (a beautiful lake in a lovely part of eastern Kentucky) and a simple conversation that changed the way I led and changed how I encouraged and motivated others. It was an "ah ha" moment for which I am grateful.

To give this story the full effect it needs, I must first give you some background information about me and one of my biggest weaknesses. I can't swim! I can do something that may resemble swimming, but under no circumstances would I be able to save myself or anyone else in an emergency. I stand a whopping five feet eight, so there are very few places where I can be in water safely. Because of my lack of ability to swim, I am very uncomfortable around water, especially water that's over my head. Even though I've received much coaching from my wife, a college roommate, two college swimming classes, and many long hours in the pool, I still struggle in water that's above my head. So as I continue with this story, it's important that I repeat that I am a very weak swimmer.

About the time when I became a principal, my wife's aunt and uncle had invited us to Lake Cumberland. We were going to spend time on the lake to boat and let our sons learn to water-ski. Most people would jump at the chance to relax, swim, and enjoy time there.

Because of my aversion to water, I had avoided this trip several times before this trip. But due to the encouragement of my family, we finally found ourselves at Lake Cumberland. Had I realized that this trip would later have such an impact on my thought process as a leader, I would have put my fears aside and been the one to plan our family vacation.

On our first day at the lake, we drove into the marina, and all that I could see was an incredibly long dock. I failed to see the beauty of the lake and all the colorful surroundings on Lake Cumberland. So as we made that unbelievably long walk down the dock to our boat, all my fears about water and swimming walked with me. I made sure that I walked squarely in the middle of the roughly eight-feet-wide and mile-long dock.

As we stood on the dock getting the boat ready and loading it for the day, my wife's uncle (Tom) must have sensed my apprehension; he made a simple statement to me that framed my career as a school administrator and all aspects of my life from that point on.

I began to hand items to Tom as he placed them inside the boat. He paused momentarily from loading the boat and said, "You know, Dan, if you're comfortable, you're not growing." That statement hit me like a ton of bricks. I'm not sure he realized the effect that his words would have on me or that they would become the inspiration for how I approach leading others to this day. Meanwhile, our families loaded the boat, and we trolled off into the lake.

I'd been searching for quite some time for a vision so that I could bring change to my school and staff. It was ironic that my own vulnerability would lead to what I now frame as my most important "ah ha" moment as a leader and as a person. I can still remember that moment and its effect on me.

That day, I kneeboarded and even rode on floats pulled by the boat. But the most important change that occurred was my vision for leadership. If I wanted to lead effectively and have a successful student-centered school, then I'd have to help people see the wisdom of the statement "If you're comfortable, you're not growing."

I wrestled with that statement for the next five days. Had I been a teacher who was just comfortable? Was I a leader who would be OK with being comfortable? How would I lead teachers and staff to move beyond their just being comfortable? What should my next steps be, and how could I lead everyone to embrace the idea that "If you're comfortable, you're not growing"?

Being comfortable leads to complacency and doing what you can to get by and not finding out who you are and what you are really capable of achieving. If you are leading others from your comfort zone, then you cannot expect them to grow (or even want to grow). So, if we want others to grow, then the growth must begin with the leader. I had to develop a plan so that I could create a mind-set in which comfortable is not OK. We needed a plan that would lead us to grow together as an organization and a family.

First, I began to tell my staff my story. I shared my fear of water and told them how I'd confronted myself and realized how important it was to constantly look for growth. I told them about my new mantra, "If you're comfortable, you're not growing," which became my theme for an entire year. Every opportunity I had, I reminded them of this mind-set and why we always needed to reach for more. Our students and parents depend on us to not be comfortable. We must be people who have high expectations of ourselves and fight to escape just being comfortable.

I shared what I had learned from my experience on the lake. First, my life jacket would help to protect me if I used it correctly, and I actually realized that I liked the water and the thrill of being pulled behind the boat; I had missed numerous opportunities in my life by being comfortable. I grew that day by being willing to move beyond my comfort zone and by trying something new.

Second, both as a staff and as an individual, we had to evaluate where we'd become comfortable. What were some of the giants that we needed to face as a staff so that we would get out of our comfort zones? Some of the areas we pinpointed involved the staff as a whole, while others involved individual leadership to face and conquer. The simple act of identifying these areas helped us to move beyond our comfort zones.

Third, we had to look deeply at the idea of accountability. As educators, we are accountable for many things, but our students' successes and failures are ultimately our greatest accountability. We began to look at other schools and how we could move beyond what was comfortable and set into motion that which would be the best for our students. Some of those changes meant creating a new mind-set, which meant planning, preparing, and putting into place our new path. Quite possibly the hardest part of this endeavor was our effort to frame how exactly we would lead our students to success.

Finally, we had to look at what we wanted our legacy to be. Were we comfortable with what our legacy was so far, both as an individual and as an organization? We had to look at our impact and decide if it had been a positive or negative impact; we then had to determine where we wanted to go from there. While the changes we made did not happen overnight, they did begin to occur—positive changes that led us to being awarded Kentucky's "school of distinction" honor.

Given the speed with which science tells us that human knowledge is doubling, it's vital that we embrace the importance of personal growth. "If you're comfortable, you're not growing" has to become our theme, regardless of our position or vocation. Aging baby boomers who are thriving have unknowingly embraced this statement. They do not fear change but instead learn to adapt and grow with the change. The sooner our younger generations learn this skill and develop strategies to grow, the more positive impact they'll have on future generations.

I have to admit that writing this book has moved me beyond my comfort zone. The process of writing has held me accountable and has made me continue to grow. Growing, motivating, and encouraging others to be lifelong learners is a legacy that I want to instill in others.

Being comfortable is the easiest route for us all. It is important that we push ourselves to engage in constant growth. We have to be aware of the moment we start to settle into a comfort zone. We have to hold ourselves accountable for our own growth and make sure that we are leaving a legacy that we'll be proud of. "If you're comfortable, you're not growing" has to become ingrained in who you are and what you do. Your accomplishments will follow.

CHAPTER 4

DON'T BE A BYSTANDER

*I always wondered why someone
didn't do something to help, then
I realized I am that someone.*

—Lilly Tomlin

ON THE JOB or just in life in general, we either choose to
participate or we watch from the sidelines. It is a choice.
In many situations, it is both important and valuable to
silently observe and to watch and learn from others' accomplishments or failures. We'll often encounter situations in which we'll need to jump in and get our feet wet.
Unfortunately, some people never get their feet wet—
they hold back from fear, lack of confidence, or complacency. Our task as leaders is to balance silent observation
with rocking of the boat.

In the early 1980s at Murray State University, Murray,
Kentucky, I had a professor named Truman Whitfield.
Dr. Whitfield was a professor everyone loved. He built

relationships by giving us real-life experiences and by connecting with his students.

Dr. Whitfield gave one of those assignments that most college students would rather not be given. It had an open-ended response, which as I recall was simply "What is one thing you would do to change public education?" I'm sure it had a minimum word limit. At that time, most writing assignments were painful for me, but this assignment intrigued me. Maybe it was because I had a specific change in mind that I wanted to make. I chose to write about traditional grading and how I believed its ineffectiveness harms education and that the system needed to be changed.

Fast-forward twenty years, and I find myself (as a principal) advocating for standards-based report cards. My staff and I began to research and implement standards-based report cards at Lone Oak Elementary. We could have stayed with the status quo (which would have been much easier), but instead we chose the path of change. We rocked the boat and chose to do something that was of paramount importance for our students.

At the beginning, standards-based reporting was something that was not comfortable for my staff or for me. We entered into a new way of assessing students, knowing that it would not be easy and that it would require us all to leave our comfort zones. We made the needs of our students our top priority, which meant that we'd always do what would be best for them.

Change, innovations, and new ideas come from rocking the boat. Accepting the status quo is not leadership: accepting the status quo is the opposite of leadership. As leaders, we have to be aware of opportunities to help change occur and to be that person who leads and does not stand in the shadows of change (or lack of change).

I believe that there are four manners in which we interact as leaders that determine if we are either bystanders or boat rockers: the Uncaring Bystander, the Confidence-Lacking Bystander, the Reluctant Bystander, and the Boat Rocker. We can find each of these archetypes in our workplaces. They inhabit our schools, offices, factories, and retail businesses. As leaders, we have to figure out how to change their thinking or motivate them to provide a more positive and productive experience.

Uncaring Bystanders are the people who may have talent and ability but for some reason have chosen to simply remain bystanders, possibly because of past experiences. They may have chosen this because of failures, or it may be because they've never been asked to move beyond being bystanders. These people may be the hardest to change.

Confidence-Lacking Bystanders are the people who simply lack the confidence to step out and rock the boat. They seem to be content just floating along. These bystanders are not going to rock the boat either through fear of failure or because they are gripped by lack of confidence. It's also possible that no one has ever encouraged them to move beyond their role as bystanders. They simply can't find the strength to do what they know to be right.

Reluctant Bystanders are similar to Confidence-Lacking Bystanders. In their case, though, they know what needs to be done—they just need others to join them or push them into doing it. They'll never confront situations or make suggestions unless they have a group to go with them to provide support. They are the people who are looking for extra encouragement and motivation as well as partners or groups to join them. They will eventually be boat rockers, but they feel safety in numbers.

Boat Rockers are the people who like fresh ideas. They are not afraid of failure and do not have to have others' participation to rock the boat. They are willing to be guinea pigs and, in many situations, they are the ones who generate ideas. They're not afraid to stand alone, and they know that rocking the boat is the right thing to do. Boat Rockers stay informed, seek growth, choose to obtain leadership positions, encourage and influence their peers, and know that taking chances may mean facing resistance.

Let me clarify that Boat Rockers are not people who cause disturbances; they're simply looking for new ideas and positive solutions that will lead to making a difference. These are people who realize the idea that "If I am comfortable, I am not growing." They are not OK with complacency, and they grow every day. They are people who face their fears and often are peer leaders.

As leaders, we have to constantly look around us to encourage people to rock the boat. We want to develop people who are seeking new ideas. We want to develop leaders who generate ideas, solve problems, and think outside the box. As the 1973 song "Rock the Boat" by the Hues Corporation also reminds us, we also can't allow the boat to tip over. It's the leader's responsibility not only to encourage boat rocking but also to prevent the organization from tipping over. As the leader, you need to keep the pulse of those new ideas and provide enough room for creativity while still being there to rein in anything that might "tip the boat over."

As I stated earlier, one crucial aspect of boat rockers' success is that they do not fear failure. The culture that surrounds them must be one that encourages risk and does not penalize failure while having the understanding that the biggest growth can come from failure.

Modeling how to rock the boat is the final part of the process to not being a bystander. For leaders to have credibility for encouraging new ideas, they must generate new ideas. The people you lead will watch to see how you as a leader will implement and carry out new ideas. They will also be watching to see what happens if your ideas are successful (as well as what happens if they fail). Remember, modeling is one of the best ways to bring about change, and keep in mind that whatever leaders do will be replicated by those whom they lead.

The second part of rocking the boat is to actually do something and not simply be a bystander or stand on the sidelines. Without actually doing something, you cannot be a Boat Rocker. You must be someone who puts your ideas into plans, your plans into action, and action into results.

Regardless of who we are, we all need to feel significant and in some way search for significance. Simply stated, we want to feel that who we are and what we do is important. We need to know that what we do matters. When we *do something*, we find our significance and realize that we are important and that we have purpose. In contrast, when we fail to do something, we struggle to find significance and purpose. When we fail to do something, we never receive the validation that we matter or that we have importance.

When we rock the boat and do something and become a doer, we begin to find our significance.

If you are a doer, you start with the decision that you are going to do something that matters. You're not going to stand on the sidelines. You make an intentional decision to accept the responsibility that it will take your actions to make change happen.

When we *do something*, we have to overcome our vulnerabilities and put ourselves out there. Being a doer means that you are willing to accept leadership.

You also have to be willing to accept criticism. With any change, criticism will inevitably follow. Be prepared, since this is part of rocking the boat and doing something that matters.

The doer connects with others and realizes that partnering and working with others is a necessity. Significance is contagious, and doers realize this. Doing something of significance will lead to a path in which others will want to become involved.

"Do something" is a simple statement. It is a rewarding statement when you act on it and actually *do something*. So this is your challenge: don't be a bystander, and don't stand on the sidelines. Do something!

CHAPTER 5

BUILDING CONFIDENCE IN YOURSELF AND OTHERS

*When we encourage people, we put
the gift of courage inside others.*

—*DAN POPE*

I BEGAN EACH day at my school in a morning assembly
with all the students. I wanted to use every moment to
build confidence, so we began and ended each assembly by reciting six positive statements. The girls would
say, "I'm brilliant, I'm beautiful, and I'm brave," while
the boys would say, "I'm smart, I'm confident, and I'm
courageous." If you were in that gymnasium and heard
our nearly six hundred students shout those positive
statements, you couldn't help but feel the confidence
shake the walls and start your day on a positive note.
Parents or visitors who joined our morning sessions often

commented that they would have liked to start their days at work on such an uplifting note.

A lack of confidence was one of the most noticeable conditions I witnessed as a school principal; I observed it in students, parents, and staff members. I saw students who lacked confidence in themselves and in their abilities. I heard parents who lacked confidence in themselves and in their abilities as parents. I observed teachers who lacked confidence in their abilities to move students forward or to do what needed to be done to help struggling students. Because this lack was so noticeable, I knew that I had to spend more time building confidence among my students, parents, and staff.

I challenge you to spend time observing those you work with (as well as friends and family) and to look for both signs of confidence and lack of confidence. A few telltale signs include posture and body language, an inability to make decisions, self-consciousness about one's appearance, negative comments about oneself, and many more. We wear our confidence visibly, for everyone to see. The signs of low self-esteem are easy to see—you just have to look and listen. If we are observant leaders, we will easily see confidence and lack of confidence in our peers, coworkers, family, and others.

I believe that lack of confidence is the biggest single reason most people never reach their potential. The absence of confidence prevents the willingness to grow and the creation of new ideas. Many people who find themselves staying comfortable and not growing simply need the basic confidence to move forward.

During the summer of 2012, I traveled with my wife to Washington, DC. Each day as we walked through Dupont Circle, we witnessed a mixture of homeless people and apparently successful people on their way to work or other destinations. The stark contrast of helplessness and assuredness made me realize that confidence (and the need for having confidence) is constantly all around us. Why did some people have confidence in their self-possession and others desperately needed a small dose of self-confidence? This experience added to my urgency to build confidence in others.

In the play *Measure for Measure*, William Shakespeare wrote, "Our doubts are traitors and make us lose the good we oft might win, by fearing to attempt." Shakespeare was talking about confidence. We fear to attempt because we lack confidence. We allow doubt and fear to be traitors in our lives instead of having faith and confidence in our abilities. So I ask you these questions: Do you have confidence? If so, do you build it in others? How do you know you have confidence? Why does it matter to those whom we lead?

A leader must have confidence, and a leader must build confidence in others. Before we can build confidence in others, we first have to develop our own self-confidence. I've identified seven characteristics that are important in developing self-confidence.

1. *Model confidence.* The simple act of modeling confidence is our first step. It may involve self-talk or intentionally showing a confident attitude; either way, doing so sets the foundation of self-confidence. Remember that as leaders, our confidence affects our leadership and those whom we lead. We cannot expect others to rely on us or to have their own confidence if we do not model self-assurance or show faith in our own abilities. Show confidence as you lead.

2. *Display ability in your leadership.* In order to be competent, we have to be prepared leaders. Being prepared goes a long way toward providing competence and confidence. Practice your skill and stay on top of your craft. Study, read, and look for your own role models to provide you with encouragement and demonstrate how you can grow as a leader. Displaying ability and being a confident leader are not easy to do; it takes work to cultivate your talents and continue to grow daily.

3. *Be positive.* Being positive goes hand in hand with confidence. Having a negative attitude kills self-confidence. Staying positive shows that you are willing to face challenges and work through problems. It is almost impossible to have confidence and not be positive. You must intentionally look for positive things around you.

4. *Make decisions.* Making decisions and being decisive will build and show confidence. If you struggle with making decisions or you second-guess your decisions, you will find it hard to be a role model for confidence. The ability to make informed decisions is the hallmark of a confident leader.

5. *Know how to handle failure.* Realize that you will fail from time to time. How you handle that failure will be one of the biggest indicators of your confidence. Show that you can cut your losses, regroup, solve problems, and then begin to move forward.

6. *Don't be arrogant.* Confidence is not arrogance. Having confidence means allowing your strengths to be seen and not being afraid of allowing others to see your weaknesses.

7. *Be genuine.* Confidence shows when we act like ourselves with others.

So why does confidence matter to the people we lead? We know that it's important to develop self-confidence, but it's just as important to build confidence in others. Encouragers make sure that they use every opportunity to build confidence in others. They not only look for opportunities but they also create opportunities to build confidence in others. I stated in chapter 2 that the word *encourage* means to place courage inside others and to give them the gift of courage. I believe that this principle also applies to confidence. Once you have confidence, you have to build it in others. The guidelines below will help you to start building confidence in others.

1. *Don't skimp on the praise.* Take every opportunity to praise people both personally and publicly. Praise often, and use specific statements that emphasize accomplishments and strengths. This praise must be authentic. If it is not authentic, people will see it as being shallow and lacking in meaning.

2. *Set goals.* When we encourage people to set goals, we are creating a path to building confidence. Setting goals gives us focus and direction that are missing when we lack confidence.

3. *Recognize the importance of failure.* Reinforce the idea that failure is an opportunity for growth. It is important to create an atmosphere in our schools, homes, and workplaces such that failure is seen as an opportunity for growth. Confidence will not be authentic if failure is not part of the equation.

4. *Provide feedback.* Feedback provides validation for accomplishments. People need reinforcement of their strengths as well as feedback about how they can improve. Feedback also shows that their leaders care.

5. *Use positive talk.* Keep the atmosphere positive, use positive talk to encourage people, and provide group encouragement. "I have confidence in you and your ability" is a statement that can help build up people and their confidence.

I cannot emphasize enough the need to build confidence in others and the necessity of seeking opportunities to build confidence in others. When we build confidence in others, we provide the ultimate encouragement and the "mountaintop" of leadership.

CHAPTER 6

DON'T LIVE FOR THE WEEKEND

*I am only one, but I am one. I cannot
do everything, but I can do something.
And I will not let what I cannot do
interfere with what I can do.*

—EDWARD EVERETT HALE

A FEW WEEKS before I retired, my staff and the parent
community surprised me by naming the school gymnasium in my honor. During our morning assembly, staff
members and parents presented me with a ceremony and
plaques to be placed in the gym. They arranged for my
family to be there and for several key people from our
central office to take part in the ceremony. The gym was
filled with staff, administrators, and almost six hundred
students. This was very humbling, but what happened
next had a tremendous effect on me and was the most
rewarding part of that morning.

As the ceremony came to a close, the staff and parents positioned me at the doorway of the gym and had my students walk past me and give me their retirement good wishes. One by one, they came to me and gave me hugs, shed tears, and left me several notes wishing me well and asking me not to retire. What happened next that morning is a moment that will be forever ingrained in my memory. One young man ran past the line, buried his head in my side and, with tears streaming, looked up at me and said, "I don't want you to go." At that instant, I realized that what I'd been trying to accomplish as a school principal really mattered to these young students. Their genuine acts of compassion had come from the climate we'd created. Not me, but what we had created together as a staff.

Each day mattered, and with the support of a tremendous staff, we made sure that every day was important and that every day had significance. We planned and made sure that every day of the week would be fun for students and staff alike. We built relationships and did not live for the weekend.

If we live our lives with the attitude that every day is important, we are giving our children and those around us a gift. Instilling the importance of each day is the gift of purpose, significance, usefulness, and of making the most of our lives. This may be one of the most important gifts we can give to anyone. I encourage you not to fall into what I call TGIF syndrome. Instead, I replace the syndrome with this statement: "Live your life as if the world would pause when you're gone."

To take this further, I believe that phrases such as TGIF, hump day, or anything that emphasizes the importance of weekends over weekdays reduces our significance. I'm not saying that we shouldn't enjoy weekends or that weekends don't refuel us, but we should enjoy every day and use every day to its fullest. When we live for the weekend, we misplace the worth of Monday through Friday and simply wish our lives away. When we're constantly waiting for the weekend, we are demonstrating to our peers, children, and those whom we lead that we really don't like our jobs or circumstances and that what we do daily is not significant. When we live for the weekend, we're not living our lives as if the world would pause when we're gone.

The next time you find yourself living for the weekend, I encourage you to evaluate your circumstances. Are you in a job that is neither purposeful nor rewarding? Do you need to change your attitude about your job? Is there something controllable that you could change about your workplace? Is it time to reinvent yourself?

Simply put, our lives are too short just to live for the weekends and not find rewards in our jobs or in helping others daily. That is the key to avoiding only living for the weekend. It is as simple as finding purpose, helping others, and seeking internal reward for what we are doing.

We have to ask ourselves these questions: Why am I doing what I'm doing? Whose day was made better because of something I've done today? If we don't have purpose, we're merely living for the weekend.

As a leader, you face many situations in which you have to be intentional and deliberate. This is also true in making sure you are not living for the weekend and that you are being purposeful. We have to deliberately work toward purposefulness. I have nine strategies to help me have purpose in my life, as noted below.

1. *Focus on helping others.* No matter what your occupation, you can find some way to make sure that you are helping someone daily. Look for opportunities to be supportive. Ask how you can aid others. It's really not hard to find ways to help people daily; as an added benefit, you'll also find it rewarding.

2. *Be an encourager.* Be that person who is the encourager in your office, home, or church. Make sure that you're adding to a positive workplace and that others want to work with you. You'll quickly find purpose by encouraging others.

3. *Be aware of your actions and attitude.* When you begin to slide into "can't wait for the weekend mode," do a self-check. Ask yourself: Is this something I can fix today? Do I need to make any adjustments to what I'm doing or the attitude with

which I approach my job? Don't allow yourself to let small circumstances turn into long-range problems.

4. *Set goals.* By setting goals, you'll create a focus on what is important. Write your goals and post them in a place where you can reflect on them daily and weekly.

5. *Make the climate fun.* The school or work climate needs to have a fun atmosphere. Research supports the notion that fun in the workplace equals or results in more success and productivity; it also creates an environment that encourages longevity with the organization. Use every opportunity you can to create and have a fun and positive day at your workplace.

6. *Enjoy family.* Make sure that you clearly communicate the importance of family—both others' families and your own. Leaders help others with those situations that often arise when people need to care for their families. Know that family situations will interfere with your own and others' days and that it's important to show empathy in those situations and provide help whenever you can.

7. *Go beyond the walls of your school or workplace.* Find ways to help the local community. Have your organization participate in volunteering and fundraising efforts to help local nonprofits. Nothing

can be more rewarding than an entire group working together to help others.

8. *Recognize value.* Remind the people in your organization of the value of the organization's goals. Make it clear that what these people are doing each day is valuable.

9. *Discourage the TGIF syndrome.* Do everything you can to discourage the TGIF syndrome. Model the opposite. Encourage Marvelous Mondays and Tremendous Tuesdays. When we create value in work or school days, we avoid the TGIF syndrome.

Life is way too short to waste it by living for the weekend. The Monday slump is just a perception that we can avoid if we recognize it and make sure that we put value in every day of the week. I challenge you to live your life as if the world would pause when you're gone. When you do, you'll stop living for the weekend and start living for every day of the week.

CHAPTER 7

A FIRE WON'T START
WITHOUT A SPARK

*In everyone's life, at some time, our inner
fire goes out. It is then burst into flame
by an encounter with another human
being. We should all be thankful for those
people who rekindle the inner spirit.*

—ALBERT SCHWEITZER

WHEN I WAS starting my career in education, I made the
decision to go back to college and work on my master's
in elementary education. The decision to work on my
master's was quite different from my experiences that
I'd had working with high-school and middle-school students. My adviser, a wise doctor in elementary education,
wanted to make sure that I would be prepared for what
was in store for me with elementary students. She made
the decision to immediately place me in a kindergarten

classroom. I quickly became connected with my students and knew that this experience would change me as a teacher.

It's been over thirty years since that experience, but I still remember its power. There was a stark difference between the attitudes of the elementary students and those of the older students toward school. My high-school and middle-school students had learned to play the game of education. Most middle-school and high-school students in my area had very little desire or passion to be at school. They were simply going through the motions and did the bare minimum to get a passing grade. The kindergarten students were completely different. They wanted to learn. I saw in them wonder, happiness, excitement, and most of all passion to learn and absorb all they could. I remember talking with different teachers and asking why the older students tended to lose their passion. Where was it going? What happened to their spark? What were we doing wrong?

The same thing happens to many of us in our workplaces. We start out with genuine passion for what we do and where we work. We are energized and believe that we're making a difference. Somewhere in the course of going about our daily routine, we lose our passion. The spark to make a difference becomes extinguished. I ask the same question: What are we doing wrong?

Having passion for what you do is a key factor for success. Many of us have passion for what we do, and many of us have lost our spark for our career or profession. Let me note that, when we've lost our passion, we're actually choosing to be average, mediocre, or run-of-the-mill. This then bleeds over into other parts of our lives. We become complacent, we stop growing, we start living for the weekend, and then we become ineffective. We lose our significance.

A few years ago, I found myself in a very stressful situation as a school principal. Our school system was heading in a direction that caused community unrest. These factors were out of my control, but I had students, staff, and parents who were relying on my leadership. We found ourselves under leadership ruled by power.

This situation had taken its toll on my passion as a school principal, and I realized that I'd allowed myself to lose my spark. Regardless of the struggles that were happening beyond the walls of my school building, I knew that I had to find my spark and my passion. I had to keep my school moving forward. My staff and students and their parents were all relying on me to lead them through this dark period in our school system.

When you struggle with trying to keep your passion and spark, you have to reflect and make a few deliberate decisions. After I made the decision not to allow the circumstances that surrounded me to interfere with my leadership, I put together a plan for myself. This was the guide that I followed:

yourself enacting more maxims like "putting out fires" and "trying to keep your head above water." Your dreams of leadership and wanting to change the world become a distant thought. If we're not careful, we can fall into the trap of day-to-day leadership. Leaders who look only at the day's problems lose their vision and goals.

I recently received a phone call from a former student. We exchanged greetings, and he congratulated me on my retirement. As we continued to talk, he explained that he'd just taken his children to school for their first day of school. He told me that as he was driving home from their school, he thought about his years in middle school. As he was reminiscing, he decided to call me. He went on to explain his accomplishments and that he had graduated from college and become a state trooper. He added that eventually he'd gone on to law school and was currently practicing law. He explained the reason for his call: he simply wanted to take the time to thank me for helping him as a student and as an athlete. We traded different stories about his years as a student and finished our conversation. Those are the moments that you as an educator live for, teach for, and are thankful for.

As I began to think about this conversation, I realized that I'd been given the opportunity to make a difference in his life. He had specifically called me to tell me that I had made a difference in his life. To make his call even more gratifying, it was evident that he was now making a difference in the lives of others.

Every day we're all given the opportunity to make a difference in the lives of others. Every day we have opportunities to help someone. Do we take those opportunities? Do we seek those opportunities? Or do we miss chances to be different and make a real difference in the lives of those we lead, our peers, and our students?

I believe that the key to being someone who makes a difference is to continue to believe that we can change the world. Yes: that we can change the world. The moment when we stop thinking that we can make a difference or stop believing that we can change the world is the moment when we begin to give up on our dreams. We begin to give up and give away a part of our significance. Mother Teresa, Martin Luther King Jr., Abraham Lincoln, and Nelson Mandela were all people who made a huge difference in the lives of others. They encountered seemingly insurmountable failures, problems, and hurdles. When we study their lives, we see that they made a difference by having faith in themselves and by knowing that with the help of others, they could change the world.

Those people also dreamed in a different way than most people do. They knew that for change to occur, they would have to change the status quo. They also believed that they could make a difference. They were leaders who knew that change keeps hope alive. And that is exactly what good leaders do: they keep hope alive. Even with insurmountable struggles, personal tragedies, and hard-fought battles, great leaders keep hope alive when others have lost every shred of their own hope.

But we have to remember that before we can make a difference, we ourselves must be different. We have to approach situations, problems, and opportunities in a different way—not just for the sake of being different, but because we truly want to be someone who makes positive changes.

So how do I know when to choose a different path to solve a problem or to avoid the status quo as a leader, peer leader, or dedicated supporter?

1. *Does it pass the "That's how we've always done it" test?* A surefire way to know if change needs to occur involves statements such as "But that's how we've always done it" or "That's just how we do it here" or even "It is what it is." To make a difference, we can't keep doing things the same old way. Being able to make a difference means finding a new path, a new way of thinking, and a new way to solve problems.

2. *Refuse to be part of the status quo.* Resist it, oppose it, and only allow the status quo to continue if it happens to be the best possible method, decision, or path. Study and do your research, then make the best decision you can. This may mean sticking with the status quo, or it may result in a whole new approach or idea.

3. *Be committed to making a difference.* Regardless of your vocation or position, be devoted to making a difference in the daily lives of others. Believe that you can change the world.

4. *Choose a good approach.* Make sure that when you choose a new approach, you have the best interests of those involved in mind. Regardless of whether those who will be affected are students, families, or employees, always make sure that the new decision or action puts their best interests first.

Before we can make a difference, we have to be different. To make a difference, we can't rely on the same old ways of doing things, the status quo, or the "that's just the way it is" mentality. When you embark on the path of a new approach, you have to remember that failure is a possibility. Whenever you try new ideas or battle the status quo, you have to be prepared that failure may be the outcome. We can't let the possibility of failure prevent us from change, however. We must remind ourselves that failure leads to learning and other opportunities. Failure is only failure when we stop trying, or it causes us to give up.

The parable of the starfish tells of a young man walking along the shore who finds thousands of starfish washed up on the beach by the tide. As he walks farther along, he sees an old gentleman picking up the starfish and throwing them into the ocean. The young man asks him what he is doing. The older gentleman replies, "The starfish will die if I don't throw them back into the ocean." The young man stops and says, "You can't possibly be able to throw enough of them back to make a difference." The older gentleman bends to pick up another starfish and throws it back into the ocean. He turns to the young man and says "It made a difference for that one."

We can change the world, and it starts with believing that we can make a difference. We have to have a plan, resist the status quo, and make sure that we are putting the best interests of others first. Just like the older gentleman in the starfish parable, "It made a difference for that one." Octave Chanute, a little-known aviator, mentored the Wright Brothers; Ezra Pound took T. S. Elliot under his wing; and Fred Birney greatly influenced Walter Cronkite. You never know what great future you may have activated by making a difference in someone's life. Be different and believe that you can make a difference in the world—in some way, somehow, for someone. Remember, "It made a difference for that one."

CHAPTER 9

EVERYONE CAN SING—YOU JUST HAVE TO FIND THE RIGHT SONG

A bird doesn't sing because it has an
answer, it sings because it has a song.

—JOAN WALSH ANGLUND

HOW MANY TIMES have you heard someone say "I can't sing" or "I'm tone deaf"? Singing and music have always been a big part of my life. I love to sing. When I hear someone say that he or she can't sing, I have a simple response: "You just haven't found the right song yet." As we go about living our lives, we should be trying to find the right song. With any luck, we'll find a song that will fit our talents and our abilities. I do believe that if you keep trying, you will find your own song.

As I said, I love to sing. Some songs I can sing easily, while others are more challenging and stretch my limits. I believe both literally and figuratively that anyone can sing—you just have to find the right song. I will use Peter Brady of *The Brady Bunch* fame as an example. In one episode, Peter Brady's voice changes during the time that the family is supposed to be recording a hit song. As the story progresses, the Brady family begins to believe that their rise to stardom is over. Then Greg, with the encouragement of his parents, solves the problem by writing a new song that incorporates Peter's changing voice as part of the song. He found the right song to fit the squeaky voice and, in true Hollywood style, the song became a hit.

I'm not saying that your squeaky voice is going to be a hit, but if you search long enough, you will find your song—and a song that you can sing and sing well.

This is also true about your life. What you do with your life is a song, and how well you sing it is up to you. You have to search to find the right song, or else you just exist. It's simple: when you're not singing your life's song, you're not living your life to its fullest.

Ask yourself: Are you singing your song? Are you using your talents and abilities to sing your best song? Are you still looking for your song? Are you spinning your wheels and wasting your time? Is your song hard to sing, and it never feels like it's your song? Are you in your life's song right now?

It is important that your song should be something you enjoy. It should be something that you find rewarding and where you are making a difference. It should be something that you can share with others and sing loudly.

So, back to my question: Are you singing your song? I challenge you to reflect right now about where you are with your career or your current situation. Are you singing your song, or do you dread going to your job each day? Do you feel like what you're doing matters and that you have a purpose? Do others look at you and know that you've found your song?

I recently traveled with my family to Florida. We boarded a three-hour flight and met a lovely young stewardess with a contagious smile who welcomed us aboard. During our time on the plane, I observed her interacting with her coworkers and the different travelers on the plane. She was intent on making sure that our flight was a pleasant and happy experience. It was apparent to me that she understood the importance of relationships and that a smile goes a long way.

As she made her way up and down the aisle, she took time to engage in conversations with several passengers. When my wife and I began to talk to her, she actually talked about having found her purpose with her job as a stewardess. She loved interacting with and helping people and making their travels a great experience. She even told us of another passenger who'd once given her a book she'd bought at a women's conference because of a conversation they'd had.

As we left the plane, I knew that she had found her song. What made this even more wonderful is the fact that she knew that she had found her song.

When you are singing your life's song, it is apparent by your actions, the way you interact with others, and how well you do your job. As I've stated in several different ways, everyone wants to find significance and purpose. We need to feel like we have a reason for being here on earth; singing our song is important to that end.

How many people do you hear each day make negative comments about their current situation or job? It's simply a job; it isn't their purpose. They are passing through life and are not living their lives as if the world would pause when they're gone.

So how do I determine if I've found my song? Take a few moments and reflect on these questions. Take time to answer them. After going through this exercise, you'll be able to reflect and determine if you are indeed singing your song.

1. Does my current situation or job have purpose?
2. Do I have opportunities to help others?
3. Do I enjoy—*really* enjoy—what I am doing?
4. Do others view my influence as having a positive impact on others?
5. Do I help others find their songs?

If you have found your life's song, keep going. Make sure that you are helping others find theirs. If, by answering these questions, you realize that you are not singing your song, then it's time to figure out why. What's keeping you from singing your song? Do you need to start planning so that you can make changes in your career or job? Do you need to reflect on how you can take your current situation and make it your song? Don't become discouraged; instead, take this as an opportunity to find your song and find your real purpose.

So what do you do if you're not singing your life's song or if you want to help someone find his or her life's song? Here are a few suggestions:

1. *Reflect on your current situation or job.* Identify why you're unhappy or not finding purpose in what you're doing. For the next few weeks, use a journal to reflect on your current situation. Write specifically about what you're doing and what effect it has on you, your family, and those around you. The act of journaling will help you frame your current situation.

2. *Identify what changes you can make to find your life's song.* Create a list of changes that you want to make in your life that will lead you toward finding your song. Prioritize the changes from the list. It may take a few days of reflection to pinpoint the changes you want to make.

3. *Take your list of changes and set a plan in place.* Include both short- and long-term goals, and decide what you need to do to successfully put these changes in place.

4. *Find an accountability partner.* Find someone to help ensure that you're working toward your goal of making the necessary changes to find your song. Choose someone whom you can confide in and who will understand what you are working toward.

5. *Make the best of your current situation or job.* Until you find your life's song, discover ways to have purpose. Purposeful change does not occur overnight, so be patient and follow your plan of finding your song.

Everyone can sing—you just have to find the right song. Wherever you are, and whatever you are doing, find your life's song. Don't just exist!

CHAPTER 10

IF YOU HAVE THE RIGHT TOOLS, YOU CAN DO ANYTHING

*If the only tool you have is a hammer, you
tend to see every problem as a nail.*

—ABRAHAM MASLOW

I GREW UP in the '60s and '70s. We were a middle-class family. My mother ran a beauty shop in our basement, and my father was a machinist and tool-and-die maker by trade. My father was a true handyman. He taught my brother and me how to repair appliances, work with wood, patch up plumbing, tinker with electricity, and build just about anything.

I can remember many Saturdays with my father spent constructing, fixing, and repairing things. He would create his list, and we'd go to the parts warehouse, hardware store, or lumberyard and find what we needed to complete our project. Once we returned home, he'd do his best to have his project done before the weekend was over.

We seldom ever called a repairman or hired someone to fix something in our home. I can close my eyes and still see my father in his work clothes measuring and getting ready to cut a board on his table saw. Today, fewer items can be repaired at home, but the lessons I learned from my father's willingness to repair things remain priceless.

When I think about those memories, I can still hear my father say, "Son, if you have the right tools, you can do anything." This may have been the most important principle that I learned during all those Saturday projects as we fixed, built, and repaired. He'd always remind us that having the right tools was vital for doing the job correctly. I can also still see his frustration when he had to rig or fudge something because he lacked the tools he needed.

In education (as in many other fields), having the right tools is crucial. We have to fill our imaginary toolboxes full of strategies, activities, and tech skills, among other things. When educators like me try to meet the needs of our students, we have to have the right tools. When we don't have the right tools, we won't move our students forward or help them reach their potential. Using the right tools with our students helps to create toolboxes for them that we can then fill with new tools.

Even if you're not an educator, using the right tools will result in additional and superior productivity. You find yourself having less frustration with your tasks. When you have the right tools in hand, you can continue to work and have less distractions or problems.

Regardless of your profession, I believe that we have and need three types of tools: social tools, tangible tools, and strategic tools. All three are important and should be found in your toolbox.

SOCIAL TOOLS

1. *Ability to build relationships.* I cannot overstate the importance of this tool. Building relationships is the key to being successful, working with others, and helping others to be successful.

2. *Portrayal of a positive attitude.* A positive attitude goes with building relationships. Presenting and having a positive attitude helps you to be more effective in working with others, and it simply helps you through the day.

3. *Knowledge of when to mediate or compromise.* In order to be productive and successful, you have to know when to compromise and when to mediate. Some situations will never change until someone is willing to compromise or help the others come to consensus.

4. *Self-motivation and the ability to motivate others.* Self-motivation as well as intentionally providing motivation for others is a tool that keeps on giving. Every aspect of our lives involves some type of motivation as well as motivating others.

TANGIBLE TOOLS

1. *Physical tools.* This can be a table saw or a screwdriver or any other tool that you need to get the job done.
2. *Technology.* Being able to use current technology and adapt to changes with technology are both imperative in today's world because of the importance of technology and how fast things change in the world of technology.

STRATEGIC TOOLS

1. *Problem-solving strategies.* You should be able to take a situation, create a possible solution, and then implement that solution.
2. *Research strategies.* Whenever you need a solution or a new idea, you need to be able to know where to look to find valuable and usable research.
3. *Creativity strategies.* You can use your creativity to start new ideas or to help move stalled ideas along.

"If you have the right tools, you can do anything." You have to approach your job and your life with this type of confidence. You have to continue to look at your toolbox and be able to replace worn-out tools, see what needs to be sharpened, and recognize what new tools you've added.

CHAPTER 11

"PRETTY GOOD" MEANS "ROOM FOR IMPROVEMENT"

I can live for two months on
a good compliment.

—MARK TWAIN

MY MOTHER IS known as the cook and baker of the family. She makes large family meals with several dishes, including salads, breads, desserts, and more desserts. She has shelves of cookbooks and has created many of her own recipes. She loves to share her creations, and we love for her to keep her kitchen cooking and baking.

Not long after my wife and I got married, we were eating a family meal with my parents when my wife asked my father what he thought about the dessert. He replied with his typical response: "Pretty good." He'd used that saying all my life, but for some reason that evening, my mother didn't appreciate his lackluster praise. She stopped what she was doing, put down her spatula, and said, "Well, Charlie, 'pretty good' means that there's room for improvement. I guess you don't like my dessert, or you must think it could be better." From that point on, if anyone in my family used the saying "pretty good," they'd be reminded that pretty good means there's room for improvement.

Praise is extremely important in all our relationships, including with family members and even in the incidental relationships that happen every day. Praise has to be genuine, and it needs to happen often. We underestimate the impact and the importance of praise. We also miss the significance of not giving praise.

I learned a valuable lesson on praise from my wife's aunt, who became a school leader about the same time I did. While we were visiting her family one summer, she took us to see the progress and new ideas she'd implemented, since she was proud of her school and its accomplishments. On one occasion, she introduced several staff members one by one to our family. These were not typical introductions. She took the time to provide genuine and specific praise about each person she introduced to us. We could see everyone's pride and self-esteem bloom as she patted each one on the back and complimented them on their strengths.

Her praise was definitely intentional. Later that day, I began a conversation with her about her introductions and the praise that she'd modeled. In our conversation, I commented that she gave specific and individual compliments for each person. We talked about how it brightened each person's day and how they all knew that she'd built relationships with them and knew something detailed about them. It was that day that I decided I had to make sure I deliberately and individually praised my staff.

I soon began to put this into practice. Whenever a visitor came to my school, I'd make a point of introducing my staff by citing specific strengths about each person. I wouldn't simply say, "This is Ms. Smith, a third-grade teacher," but "This is Ms. Smith, who recently received her National Board Certification; she's very dedicated, and a student of hers recently won a local essay contest." I'd try very hard to have three specific ways to praise each person in front of visitors.

Making sure that I used specific praise had an immediate and positive impact. It was apparent that my staff enjoyed being praised in public. What was even more apparent was that they enjoyed the fact that I knew specific things to praise them about in public. So back to the title of the chapter: imagine if I used the term "pretty good" to describe a teacher or staff member when I introduced him or her to a visitor. I'm "pretty" sure it would have had the opposite effect.

Praise also needs to be done in writing. You can use notes, cards, letters, and even e-mail to provide praise.

Early on in our marriage, my wife taught at a local elementary school. She came home one day after a classroom-observation session and mentioned that her principal always left notes of praise after each classroom observation. The principal's notes were positive and specific about the strengths of the teachers' lessons and always ended by thanking the teachers for their service to the school. When I became a principal myself, my wife encouraged me to use this same idea.

After my first year as a principal, I began to realize the effect of this strategy when I noticed that teachers kept their notes posted on their desks and their bulletin boards. We often overlook the fact that something as simple as a positive note can have such an effect on people.

The following principles will help make sure that providing praise becomes part of your leadership toolbox.

1. *Praise needs to be genuine.* "Pretty good" is an example of empty praise. We dispense empty compliments every day when we are just being polite. If we are not in the habit of providing genuine praise to people, then it will not happen.
2. *Praise has to be deliberate.* We have to make a conscious effort to praise people daily. Create a reminder to yourself to help prompt you to praise people daily, and make praising daily a habit.
3. *Praise in private, and praise in public.* We need to be told to praise face-to-face as well as in group settings.

4. *Praise needs to be timely.* When someone does something good, be timely in providing praise. If too much time elapses, the effect of the praise will be empty.

5. *Don't leave anyone out.* It's very hard—but also very important—not to leave anyone out. Make sure that you provide praise to all who should receive it.

6. *Don't praise people if they don't deserve it.* When we praise people who don't deserve it, we lose credibility with others.

CHAPTER 12

RELATIONSHIPS

*You can make more friends in two months
by becoming interested in other people
than you can in two years by trying to
get other people interested in you.*

—DALE CARNEGIE

WHEN I WAS young, wherever we traveled, we'd always encounter someone who knew my father. It actually became a running joke with my mother and brother to see if we could go somewhere and *not* run into someone he knew. If we did not run into an acquaintance or old friend, he would make a new friend.

He was by no means famous, nor did he have a job that made him widely recognizable. He had the ability to strike up conversations and make connections with everyone he met. In a short time, he would be telling stories and making new friends. He knew the importance of interactions, and he'd mastered the art of building relationships.

As a child, I was apprehensive about my father's un-canny ability to talk with anyone. Because I was a very shy child, for some reason his behavior embarrassed me. Both my parents were very outgoing, but from an early age, I struggled with talking to others. Now that I'm an adult, I appreciate my father's extraordinary ability to talk to any stranger, and I try to be just like him. I want to pass that quality on to my children. It's important—very important—to be able to talk to people and connect with them and give them a small part of you.

When I began my career as a principal, I made every attempt I could to build relationships. I had a small round table in my office that I called my listening table. When someone came to my office, I would stop whatever I was doing, we would sit at the listening table, and I would give him or her my undivided attention. Unfortunately, after a few years, I stopped using the table and often had to be re-minded to make sure to listen and direct my focus to those who needed to talk with me. My listening table helped me to focus on the person and the conversation that we were having. If I had the chance to begin my career again, I'd have a listening table and would never stop using it.

Numerous books have been written about building relationships being the key to success in every facet of our lives, including family, career, and everything else. If we can't build relationships, we will struggle. Everything we do is connected to relationships and our ability (or inability) to build strong relationships.

If you study current or past leaders, you'll see that very few of them have been successful without being relationship builders. The aforementioned James Comer stated that "no significant learning occurs without a significant relationship." American botanist and inventor George Washington Carver said that "all learning is understanding relationships." I'll take this idea further and say that nothing of significance occurs without a meaningful relationship.

I encourage everyone to aspire toward being a "people person." You should add this trait to your toolbox. Being a model relationship builder can set a great example for our children, students, friends, or coworkers. We should be working daily to build relationships that are meaningful and positive and modeling this skill for everyone we come in contact with.

Successful schools, businesses, and other organizations have found the importance of relationship building. They have harnessed its potential to bring people together to accomplish goals, create new ideas, and generally make life better. Many people have accomplished this success through creating a sense of family and community within their organizations.

If you want to be truly successful as a leader, you cannot just stop at building relationships. You must be able to create that sense of family and community with the people you lead. That sense has to be part of the culture. You have to put it in place and set the example.

It is the leader's responsibility to create and nurture a sense of family and community. When an organization has a sense of connection and family, it will thrive. Organizations that have this culture will survive adversities and maintain a positive outlook, while those that don't will struggle when difficulties arise.

Everything we do is affected by the relationships we build and the time that we invest in others. Relationship building is undoubtedly our best use of time and energy. The adage "A man reaps what he sows" can truly be applied to building relationships. If we build positive and strong relationships, we will reap good fruit.

Building relationships grows into creating family and community. The workplace must have a sense of family and community to reach its potential. When leaders intentionally create an atmosphere of family and community, they are creating a place where people want to work and they take pride in their daily activities.

So how do you get there? It will not happen overnight, and you may need to put time and energy into developing your people skills. It will also mean using deliberate actions and scheduling specific events that have certain intent to build relationships.

From my experiences as a leader, the following items are the habits I encourage you to put into practice that will help you to become a relationship builder. You must remember that this will not happen overnight, but implementing these habits will gradually result in strong and fruitful relationships.

1. *Invest time in people.* Spend time with your family, friends, and the people you work with.
2. *Be present and be involved.* Put down your phone, iPad, or whatever else might be a distraction. Create something like my listening table that will provide a distraction-free time to have meaningful conversations.
3. *Greet and speak to everyone every day.* Even if you just greeted someone an hour ago, take the opportunity to recognize him or her and have a conversation. Eye contact and a friendly face are imperative.
4. *Laugh, cry, and rejoice.* Our emotions are crucial in building relationships. Our emotions connect us. Our emotions create bonds that bring relationships to the sense of community and family that we're looking for.
5. *Listen.* Being a good listener is a tool we all need to build relationships. If you're too busy to listen, then you'll automatically build walls that will prevent you from building relationships.
6. *Be genuine.* Just be you. Be the same person with everyone. People always recognize a fake personality.
7. *Be the positive person in the room.* Healthy, productive relationships are built on positivity. Negativity will only attract people who choose to be negative.

8. *Show respect.* Show and give respect to others. Without respect, there is no foundation for a healthy relationship to be built.
9. *Be honest.* If you are not honest, people will think you're building relationships just for personal gain.
10. *Find ways to connect.* Connect with your groups through common interests, activities, and hobbies. We all have at least one common interest or way in which we can connect. It may take hard work and a lot of time, but even the hardest shell can be cracked.
11. *Have meetings and gatherings.* Schedule these times with the sole purpose of building relationships.
12. *Let people know that you care.* Be sure to tell people that you're available to help in times of need.

In any situation, the foundational skill for success is the ability to build relationships. Success in parenting, friendships, occupations, and leadership relies on your ability to build and sustain relationships. If we hold to the statement that nothing of significance occurs without significant relationships, then put your energy into building and sustaining them. Greatness will follow.

CHAPTER 13

NEVER STOP LEARNING AND GROWING

*Anyone who stops learning is old, whether
at twenty or eighty. Anyone who keeps
learning stays young. The greatest thing
in life is to keep your mind young.*

—HENRY FORD

ACCORDING TO THE researcher David Russell Schilling, scientists have stated (as I alluded to earlier) that civilization is now doubling human knowledge every thirteen months. He further states that scientists also once believed that human knowledge doubled every century; then, after World War II, our knowledge began to double every twenty-five years. Schilling believes that the Internet is responsible for the currently rapid increase in knowledge. Astonishingly, IBM predicts that human knowledge will soon double every twelve hours.

I find it hard to wrap my brain around the concept of doubling human knowledge. It is an amazing thought that we have this much information available to us. It also sets up the scenario that in order to flourish, we must always keep learning and growing.

I grew up before the time of the personal computer. I can remember my parents and many adults saying "I don't need a computer" or "I'll never use one." During the beginning of the computer age, many people refused to embrace the changes that were occurring as early technology tiptoed its way into our daily lives. Many people were afraid of having to learn something new. Others simply refused to have anything to do with early computers. Today, most aspects of our lives involve the use of some type of computer technology; unless you live under a rock, you have to use some form of computer technology.

I've noticed in my observations of older adults that those who continue to thrive have realized the importance of continuing to learn and to be lifelong learners. Thriving older adults do not avoid learning new things or using technology. In my observations, seniors who use their iPhones or other technology and are willing to continue to learn new things want to thrive and flourish. They continue to be productive and alive, both socially and emotionally. They keep their minds and bodies flourishing by simply being lifelong learners.

The Spanish explorer Juan Ponce de León searched for many years for the fountain of youth. According to historical accounts, he never located the fountain, because we know that it doesn't actually exist. The twenty-first-century fountain of youth does exist, however. If you embrace the principle of lifelong learning and strive to never stop growing intellectually, emotionally, and socially, your mind will stay young and alive. I believe that lifelong learning is crucial for us to thrive throughout our entire lives.

Whether you're twenty or a hundred, the idea of being a lifelong learner is equally important. When we close our minds to the idea of learning, we stop flexing one of our most important muscles: the brain. Creativity, problem solving, curiosity about finding new information, and flexibility to do things in different ways will all spring from lifelong learning. Motivation, purpose, self-esteem, and significance can quickly develop within us as we learn and set goals to continue to learn. Who doesn't want these characteristics in their lives?

When we embrace the idea of being lifelong learners and become committed to the pursuit of continual learning, we'll have the opportunity to be productive our entire lives. So how can we get on track to becoming lifelong learners? Here's how.

1. *Practice self-motivation.* You will not become a lifelong learner unless you're motivated to want to continue to learn or to learn something new.

2. *Collaborate with others.* According to Ecclesiastes 4:9, "Two are better than one because they have a good return for their labor." Join a group (or start a group) that focuses on something you're interested in learning more about, or learn something new. Collaboration is a tool that opens doors. Research supports the notion that two heads are better than one and that collaboration leads to new opportunities.

3. *Read.* A teacher who mentored me in my early career told me that "reading is the key to all knowledge." Read as much as you possibly can about new topics or topics that you want to learn more about. Read, and then read some more.

4. *Attend a class/seminar or learn online.* Connect with podcasts and create a web page.

5. *Develop new skills.* Whatever your career is, it's good practice to continually develop new skills.

6. *Write.* Develop your writing skills and share your writings in some format.

7. *Research a new topic.* Set a goal to become an expert in that area.

8. *Start a new hobby.* We all have hobbies that we've always wanted to do but never had time for. There's no time like the present.

9. *Study opposing views.* By doing so, you'll be able to understand where other people's points of view originate.

10. *Listen.* Whether it's TED talks or some other venue, develop your listening skills. Listen for the sake of learning.

11. *Set goals for lifelong learning.* If you've made it this far in *If You're Comfortable, You're Not Growing*, you've made a step forward in becoming a lifelong learner. Take the chapters in this book to set goals for your path to growth. Each chapter is focused on moving beyond your comfort zone; an underlying theme of the book is for you to continue to grow and learn. Set your goals and do everything you can to thrive your entire life.

CHAPTER 14

SHOUT IT FROM THE ROOFTOPS-DANCE, SING, AND CELEBRATE

*Find your voice, shout it from the rooftops,
and keep doing it until the people
that are looking for you find you.*

—DAN HARMON

TEST SCORES HAVE become a stressful part of schools' and principals' accountability. A few years ago, my superintendent asked me how I communicated the results of my tests scores. Anticipating that our school would do well, I said, "Shout it from the rooftops." After weeks of waiting and anticipation, the day finally came in which our test scores were publicized. We were top in the district and had earned one of the top scores in the state.

I wanted to do something unexpected to surprise my staff and students and their parents. My wife reminded me of my comment about shouting it from the rooftops.

As always, she wanted to help me celebrate our success. She suggested that I climb to the top of the school roof and, as students and staff entered the building, do what I said I'd do and *shout it from the rooftops*.

That is exactly what I did. Armed with multiple signs, I walked out on the roof where I would be easily visible. When parents dropped off their sons and daughters and staff members entered the building, I shouted our success from the rooftops and praised our students and staff. It became a tradition for the next few years as we continued to be listed among the top schools in the state.

Shouting it from the rooftops may seem extreme, but doing so emphasizes those big events and accomplishments that require tremendous applause. You don't have to literally stand on the roof to shout it from the rooftops; you could stand on a chair in a meeting or use a megaphone in the hallway to get your message across. You have to broadcast those big events. People must see their leaders as being excited and exuberant about their accomplishments.

Shouting it from the rooftops combines the simplicity of the town crier with energy and excitement and will have a more far-reaching impact than you might expect. Whether you're talking about employees, students, parents, or family members, shouting it from the rooftops confirms the significance of what people have been working toward.

I really enjoy the Christmas season, and one of my favorite holiday stories is Charles Dickens's *A Christmas Carol*. In that story, Dickens describes the character Mr. Fezziwig as being the antithesis of Ebenezer Scrooge. Mr. Fezziwig is the "shout it from the rooftops" character. In *A Christmas Carol*, it is apparent that he is a man of kindness and generosity who has affection for his employees. Mr. Fezziwig's character gives us a great example of the importance of dancing, singing, and celebrating with the people we work with and work for.

In an earlier chapter, I mentioned our school's morning assemblies and the impact these had on my students, staff, and parents. During morning assembly, we danced, sang, and celebrated. We would shout out our accomplishments to the point that it would be almost impossible to leave the morning assembly not feeling ready and excited about the day ahead.

Reflect on the past few weeks. Did any of your days have any "woo-hoo!" moments? Did you take part in celebrating success or take a moment to sing and dance about something exciting? If you did have times of celebration, then keep those times going. Share them and make them multiply. If your past few days and weeks did not include opportunities for celebration, then it's time to add such moments to your day.

CHAPTER 15

LEAVING A LEGACY– OPPORTUNITY OR OBLIGATION?

Are we being good ancestors?

—Jonas Salk

When you reach milestones in your life, you might become reflective. Retirement, marriage, a new job, a new career, the birth of a child, or whatever the milestone, these landmarks in our lives cause us to pause and reflect on our legacy. Are we where we want to be in our lives? Have we reached the goals we wanted to reach? What's our next step? What should we do now? These are questions that we ask ourselves whenever we reach these landmarks.

In 2016, as I mentioned in the introduction, I retired as a school principal. I loved my job; it was my dream job. I left at the pinnacle of my career. Leading up to the last days, I became very reflective about my thirty-two years in education. I questioned myself about my accomplishments and deliberated about whether I'd reached all my goals. I reminisced about the people I'd worked for and worked with as well as the relationships I'd built. Had I done everything that I could have done?

The most important question that I kept asking myself was if I had made a difference. Throughout my career, had I made a lasting impression on the people I worked with? Most importantly, I wanted to know if I'd made a difference in the lives of the older students and younger children who were under my care.

The question I was really asking myself was what my legacy would be as a teacher, coach, and principal. I wasn't concerned about accolades. I wanted to make sure that I'd set a good example, made good decisions (and for the right reasons), and positively changed students' lives.

By writing this book, I've tried to encourage the notion that helping others and leaving a positive legacy are extremely important. I've described several ways to develop personally and to help others. All the chapters will lead you toward success either personally or vocationally or through building relationships.

With that said, a major goal of this book is to redefine the definition of success. Success should be based on helping others daily and not expecting anything in return. It doesn't matter what your position, occupation, or education is: you can still find people who need help, whether it's with something small or with helping them to get their lives back on track.

If we simply open our eyes and our ears, we'll find multiple opportunities to be successful daily based on my definition of success. Help other people. Your legacy will be tremendous if you adopt this definition of success.

So what is your legacy at this point in your life? Regardless of your occupation or your place in life, take a moment and think about the legacy that you're crafting. Are you where you want to be in your life? Have you accomplished your goals? Are you helping someone every day?

Remember, it's never too late to shape a positive legacy. It's never too late to implement change, get out of your comfort zone, and change your small corner of the world, nor is it ever too late to live your life as if the world would pause when you're gone.

Is your day an opportunity or an obligation? You have a daily choice to make. Are you just going through the motions, or are you seeking opportunities to help someone? It's really that simple. If you observe people, you can tell very quickly if they look at their day as an opportunity or an obligation.

In chapter 9, I told a story about a flight attendant who found her song as a stewardess. It was clear to me that she viewed her job as an opportunity to help others; she didn't look at it as an obligation. As she made her way down the aisle of the plane, she used her relationship skills to greet and help my fellow passengers on the plane. Watching her interact with the passengers put a smile on my face. She had such an impact on the passengers during our flight that one passenger even gave her a book she'd recently bought. From my experience, it's not often that passengers show their appreciation to the flight attendants; she used her short time on the plane as an opportunity to help and to have an impact on others.

The moment your feet hit the floor in the morning, you have to make the decision: Is this going to be a day of obligation or opportunity?

My family likes to have big holiday meals with plenty of leftovers, whether it's Christmas, Thanksgiving, Easter, birthdays, or anything else. Several years ago, I began to take plates of leftovers to the clerks at a local convenience store, since I was concerned that they might be missing meals with family and friends because they had to work during the holidays. This has become a tradition. After we eat and have dessert, we prepare a smorgasbord for my friends at the store. They're always very appreciative, and I enjoy the satisfaction of doing something for someone while expecting nothing in return.

It's an opportunity to help and build relationships. It could easily become an obligation or tradition that I just do to go through the motions. Instead, I use that time to thank them for helping me and my fellow customers each day; I recognize that they have to celebrate the holidays while working at the convenience store.

In order to make sure that you're pursuing opportunities and lessening your obligations, you have to have deliberate strategies in place.

1. Make the decision to look for opportunities; avoid falling into the obligation rut.
2. Look at every interaction with others as an opportunity to build a positive relationship, whether it's with family, friends, the people you work with, or those brief moments in your day when you encounter people at the store, on the phone, or in the parking lot.
3. Set a goal to help someone every day.
4. Volunteer in organizations whose sole purpose is to help others.
5. Seize the moment. When opportunities land in your lap, do something now. It may be as simple as carrying a package for someone, making a phone call to help someone in need, or helping an elderly person put groceries in the car.
6. Don't allow something to become an obligation. When something starts to feel like an obligation, prevent that from occurring. Reflect on why you're doing what you're doing. Find positive reasons that will make it an opportunity instead.
7. When something becomes an obligation, it may be time to make a change.

This chapter on leaving a legacy is one of the most important chapters in this book. Using these strategies and those discussed earlier will help lead you to a rich, successful legacy of helping others. These strategies can become part of your daily life and can help you to become someone who makes opportunities and turns obligations into opportunities.

CHAPTER 16

ASK GOOD QUESTIONS AND BE A GOOD LISTENER

The important thing is not to stop questioning.
Curiosity has its own reason for existing.

—ALBERT EINSTEIN

ONE OF THE most overlooked skills for leaders, teachers, and those in most other professions is the skill of asking questions. The power of questioning is widely underestimated. We usually don't ask enough questions. We struggle with asking good questions or even choosing the right questions.

I love Voltaire's advice to "judge a man by his questions rather than by his answers." He's telling us that questions can be more important than our answers and that questions can lead us to gaining more knowledge.

Since asking questions leads us to having more knowledge, we need to spend time developing our questioning skills. We need to learn how to develop questions, build on other questions, and much more. Then, we need to encourage others to develop their questioning skills.

When we look at children, we find that they are innately questioners. As soon as children develop the ability to speak in sentences, the questions begin to flow. Somewhere in the early teens, our questioning stops or slows down dramatically. Unfortunately, adults (including parents and teachers) do more to stifle questioning than to encourage students and children to ask questions. Why does this occur? Why do we not do more to inspire questioning? Why do our schools not urge questioning? Why do our organizations not use questions to encourage creativity and innovation?

Are we afraid of questions? Are we afraid of where they might lead us? Are we worried that we won't be able to provide answers? The answer could be that questions can make us uncomfortable. We have to be willing to say, "I don't know the answer, but we can find out."

Questions lead to creativity, inventions, and new ideas. New ideas and inventions lead to added questions and then spark more creativity. Some examples of how creativity grew out of questions include Kellogg's Corn Flakes, plastics, artificial sweeteners, microwave ovens, and the discovery of x-rays. Because of creativity, the questions sparked new inventions, and discoveries were born.

Good leaders ask questions. They ask questions for others and they ask questions for themselves. They cannot be afraid to ask questions or to allow others to ask questions. True leadership encourages inquiry and provides opportunities for others to ask open and honest questions.

How should you ask more questions and encourage others to do the same? Here's how.

1. Realize that questions can be simple. They do not have to be deep, thoughtful inquiries; they can be as simple as "Why do we do it this way?" or "How can we change what we're doing?"
2. Study the art of asking questions. A large body of knowledge exists on asking questions. The author Warren Berger's website A More Beautiful Question is a great resource that's full of valuable information about the art of questioning.
3. Start meetings or group activities by asking questions.
4. Set aside a location for others to post any questions they may have.
5. If you can't answer a question, just admit it. Then, work to find an answer.

Once you begin to stimulate your own questioning and the questioning of others, listening is the next important skill to employ and develop. Many leaders, parents, and peers overlook this skill, yet the power of listening is extraordinary. Without the skill of listening, questioning will lose its effectiveness.

First, when we ask others questions, we have to learn that silence and patience are vital if thoughtful answers are to be forthcoming. We often ask a question and expect an immediate response, which may not produce the creativity and discovery we're hoping for. A person who's been asked a good question needs to let it soak in for a while as he or she ponders a response. Listening involves patience.

Second, we have to listen to the responses we receive. Listen to what the other person is saying, and look for other questions that may be hidden in their responses. Be able to reply to their answers by explaining what you've just heard them say. This will allow the response to soak in, and it validates the fact that you were listening.

So, are you asking questions? Are you listening? Asking questions and listening both open doors that may currently be closed or not there at all. Take the opportunity to reflect on your own questioning and see how you can improve. What questions are out there waiting for you?

CHAPTER 17

MORE WORDS OF WISDOM

*Do not go where the path may lead, go instead
where there is no path and leave a trail.*

—RALPH WALDO EMERSON

I'M SURE YOU'VE heard the term "communication overload," which refers to having too much information and not being able to process it. We've all been in situations in which we can't process all that's being communicated to us, but I believe that if we use communication effectively, wisely, and in a timely manner, we can never have enough communication.

My faculty heard me say that exact statement many times: "You can never have enough communication." We provided a newsletter, e-mails, a website, phone messaging, fliers, and many other forms of communication, but I never felt we'd ever provided enough information to our parents, students, and staff.

I had a newsletter for parents that we e-mailed twice a month to the school's parents and the wider community. I was able to track how many people actually opened these e-mails and was surprised to find that only 30 percent of the parents took the time to read them. I knew this meant that we had to make sure that we used multiple forms of communication.

I used a rule of three as the minimum for any type of communication. If we had important information that needed to be broadcast, I made sure that we used at least three forms of communication. Although the information appeared in different formats, the information was the same. Yes, we'd always have someone say that they didn't get the information or that they knew nothing about it, but that simply reinforced my belief that you can never have enough communication.

Below are a few other pieces of advice I've picked up over the years.

DON'T COMPLAIN

We all know people who spend their days being negative. They believe that the world is out to get them. I call this the Eeyore syndrome. These people are constantly unhappy and spend their time trying to take everyone with them. Every office, family, team, or group has a person who suffers from the Eeyore syndrome: the sky is falling, the weather is bad, I'll never get this done, it always happens to me. We've all fallen into this trap, but doing so doesn't help us or make us more productive. It actually makes us feel worse and will increase our anxiety and stress.

We complain for many reasons: we could do it out of habit, we could do it to control others, or we could do it out of jealousy. Complaining simply doesn't help.

When complaining becomes part of your organization, group, or family, you need to address the problem. Make the complainer aware that he or she is being heard, but point out that this could be done in more productive ways. Here are a few other tips related to complaining:

1. Designate complain-free zones.
2. Create an avenue in which complaints can be expressed.
3. Give people an accountability partner to allow them to vent, but also make them accountable for any negativity that their complaints may cause.
4. Be a model for having a complaint-free attitude.

DO THE RIGHT THING FOR THE RIGHT REASON

Often when you've successfully dealt with seemingly impossible circumstances, you'll realize that those difficult circumstances had become opportunities. This is especially true when you are doing what is right.

We're faced with decisions every day: simple decisions, decisions that will affect us for a long time, and decisions that will only have short-term consequences. Some very important decisions even affect people's lives. Unfortunately, not all decisions are the best possible decision, nor are they always done for the right reason.

If you've ever had to make a decision that would upset someone's life, you know that such decisions are not easy to make. You have to choose and decide which decision will be best for everyone involved. If you have a conscience—and we all do—making hard decisions can be daunting. You want to do the right thing for the right reason.

NO ONE PLANS ALONE

In education, planning is a vital part of doing what's best for the students. You can do school-wide planning, grade-level planning, and planning in the classroom. I quickly learned that allowing staff members to be islands unto themselves would not be productive for anyone. Doing so causes distrust and unwanted competition, it creates an unproductive sense of independence, and it's not good for student growth.

My staff soon often heard the statement "no one plans alone." Just like the saying "two heads are better than one," planning together is more productive than planning alone. It also requires people to work together as a team, which builds trust and creates transparency.

CHAPTER 18

FINAL ANALYSIS

*Give the best you have, and it will never
be enough. Give your best anyway.*

—MOTHER TERESA

MY FATHER OFTEN surprised us with unexpected talents. At some point in my early teens, I discovered that he loved poetry. He didn't fit the mold of someone who would enjoy poetry, but out of the blue, he'd often recite lines from his favorite poems. He'd memorized several poems, and if the situation sparked his inner troubadour, he'd recite a few lines.

One poem in particular he'd recite was the poem "If," by Rudyard Kipling. We studied the poem in my eighth-grade English class, and I quickly made a connection. I didn't understand the meaning of the poem at the time, but it did make me feel confident and hopeful for my future. I was unaware that the poem would have a lasting effect on me.

Through the years, I'd often remember certain lines of the poem; I even kept a copy so that I could hear my father recite his favorite lines again and reconnect with that same confidence and hope I'd experienced when I was younger.

Here are the first lines of the poem: "If you can keep your head when all about you / Are losing theirs and blaming it on you." Whatever your leadership position—as a CEO, a teacher, a lawyer, or even a parent—keeping your head when all about you are losing theirs is sound advice. Kipling tells us how to deal with doubt, waiting, lies, and hatred. He also tells us not to be bothered by what others think about us and to avoid creating un-healthy relationships.

The next part of the poem focuses on how we greet the world: how we dream and think, how we meet tri-umph and disaster, and whether we fight on or just give up. He encourages us to never give up. We must "Hold on!" He concludes the poem with an examination of how we grapple with failure and how we should treat one an-other. I find it impossible to read the poem without be-ing motivated to give and do my best.

Years later, while I was trying to find motivation for my staff and for myself, I ran across the words of Mother Teresa that she's thought to have written on a wall in Calcutta: "Do It Anyway."

"If" and "do it anyway" are both convincing words of encouragement that provide advice for achieving true success. Both fit my new definition of success (related to helping others) that I presented in chapter 15.

There are several variations of the "do it anyway" lines, and there's even some speculation about whether they truly were Mother Teresa's words, but this does not take away their impact. When I discovered this writing, I quickly made a connection with "If." The words of both Kipling and Mother Teresa provide strong advice for leaders and convincing advice for anyone else. I was so encouraged by these writings that I kept a copy of both posted in my office. I would read them both for inspiration during those times when I needed to make hard decisions, whether I wanted to make sure I was making the right decisions for the right reasons or simply needed a reset for my moral judgment.

The words "do it anyway" have a strong focus on our relationships with others. They tell us to forgive, succeed, be kind, be honest, be happy, do good, and give the best we have; even though you may not be encouraged by others, "do it anyway." I challenge you to read Mother Teresa's words; I promise that you'll feel the same encouragement I did.

The Bible and Matthew West's song "Do Something" were two other encouragers that I often used to keep me feel uplifted during my career. I kept a copy of the *Maxwell Leadership Bible* on my desk and did my best to read from it daily. It helped to keep me focused on my faith and on being a servant leader. I wanted people to see my faith in my leadership. They needed to see me extend grace and hope and encouragement to others. I wanted them to know that how I made my decisions and how I approached leadership were directly related to my faith in God.

West recorded "Do Something" while I was in the last two years of my career as a principal. The song became my "earworm" that replayed over and over in my head. Two lines in the song—"But we're never gonna change the world by standing still" and "Right now it's time to do something"—kept me moving forward and doing everything I had in me to do what was best for my students, staff, and school.

All of us, including leaders and those who are led, have to have something that motivates and inspires us. I've described in this book the things I used during my career to give me that internal motivation. What can you find that will help you live your life as if the world will stop when you're gone? What is it that will cause you to rock the boat, make a difference, build confidence, be the spark, find your song, stop being comfortable, and yes, change the world?

I hope that I've encouraged you to go and instill courage in others. Remember: if you're comfortable, you're not growing.